"The Winding Roads"

Poems and Postcards
of
County Down

compiled by

Jack McCoy

Blackstaff Press

For kind permission to reprint copyright material, the following acknowledgements are made:

To William Mullan & Son for poems by 'John o' the North' (Harry T. Browne) and for a poem from Padraic Gregory's book; to the Headley Bros. of Invicta Press for Mary Lowry's extract; to Arthur H. Stockwell for a poem by Amanda McKittrick Ros; to the Editor of the *Belfast Telegraph* for the article on Crawfordsburn Inn; to the Editor of the *Mourne Observer* for William Rowan's poem; to Mrs Eileen Boyd, daughter of the poet, for John Moore's poem; to Mrs Wyn Fisher for Lynn Doyle's poem; to Mr Michael Williams, the poet's son, for poems by Richard Rowley, and to Dundalgan Press for the inclusion of Rosamund Praeger's poem.

I wish also to extend thanks to Mr D. H. Welch, Chief Librarian of the South Eastern Library Service, for permission to use the material and facilities of the Special Collection at Library Headquarters, to Mr J. R. R. Adams, Librarian of the Linen Hall Library, for help and co-operation, and to my colleagues for their sufferance.

To John Hewitt too I am grateful for supplying information on many of the writers represented; to Tim Collins of the Library, University College, Galway, for information on Rosamund Praeger, and to Bill Pollock for queries answered.

I am indebted also to the manager of the Tropicana Motor Hotel, Los Angeles, and to Jim Jenkins, who showed interest.

(Every effort has been made to trace the owners of copyright material used in this book. In the event of omission the publisher would be glad of notification.)

British Library Cataloguing in Publication Data

McCoy, Jack
 The winding roads.
 1. County Down — Literary collections
 808.8'03'2   PN6071.I/

ISBN 0-85640-243-5

© Jack McCoy, 1980

Published by Blackstaff Press Limited, 3 Galway Park, Dundonald, Belfast, BT16 0AN.
All rights reserved. No part of this publication may be reproduced, stored in a retrieval system, or transmitted, in any form or by any means, electronic, mechanical, photocopying, recording or otherwise, without the prior permission of Blackstaff Press Limited.

Conditions of Sale: This book shall not without the written consent of the Publishers first given be lent, re-sold, hired out or otherwise disposed of by way of trade in any form of binding or cover other than that in which it is published.

ISBN 0 85640 243 5

Printed in Great Britain by Richard Clay (The Chaucer Press) Ltd, Bungay, Suffolk.

Contents

Introduction

Down county was for long the darling of the Victorian and Edwardian sight-seer, traveller and professional invalid.

Its eccentric topography was the sort in fashion at the time — not quite the unfettered wildness beloved by the earlier Romantics, but a more modest, manageable version, still of a scale to stimulate and please, but not overtax, the nineteenth-century sensibility. That doughty dame-traveller of Ireland, Mrs S. C. Hall remarks thus:

> The county is remarkable for its inequality of surface; for although the mountains are chiefly confined to the southern district, where they are magnificent, the lesser hills are abundant in all parts; hence it is said to have derived its ancient name 'Dunum' which signifies a hill, or a hilly country. This peculiar character — a perpetual rise and fall of the land-scape — renders it highly picturesque.

Holidaymaking in the seaside towns and inland health spots, although increasing in popularity during the early years of last century, took off rapidly after 1846 when the Belfast and County Down Railway arrived. The first Railway Act of that year authorised the construction of a line from Belfast to Downpatrick with branches to Holywood, Newtownards, Bangor and Donaghadee. Further lines were made from Comber to Ballynahinch and by 1866 a line was built from Downpatrick through Dundrum to Newcastle. In addition, a coastal coach route connected the rail terminus at Newcastle with Rostrevor and Warrenpoint through Kilkeel. By 1924 the Company claimed to be carrying ten million passengers a year over eighty miles of track.

Although the excuses for tripping to the sea were usually to do with ill-health, actual or imagined — it was not yet thought altogether proper to take a holiday just to enjoy yourself — it was obvious even to Dr Knox (erudite champion of the diluent, diaphoretic, relaxant and emetic properties of the waters of sea and spa and of the salubrious qualities of fresh bracing air) that there were other, more sociable aspects to the fortnight's 'break':

> Proper division of the day, cheerful conversation, interesting books, botanical and geological excursions, regular and moderate exercise short of exhaustion, and early retirement to rest, are all points well worthy of attention in order to make our time pass lightly on, and to guard against ennui, the most unfailing attendant of idleness.

And so, swayed by the weighty exhortations of the physicians, the exuberant advertisements of the transport companies and the fluent praise of the guide books, the visitors jaunted the highways and byways of scenic interest and flocked to the booming resorts, by now full of grandiloquent hotels and buoyant guest houses. Attractions for the tourist were as numerous as the sands on a crowded beach. For the sketcher alone the BCD&R handbook outlined these delights:

County Down is a capital district for artists and photographers, being unusually well provided with railways and other modes of conveyance traversing all the finest scenery in the district. At Helen's Bay and Craigavad are many good seaside bits, easily accessible from either Belfast or Bangor; whilst points on the Castlereagh hills offer striking views of the wide and fertile valley of the Lagan. Passing out of Belfast Lough from Bangor, the little harbour of Groomsport, and many capital rocky bits looking on the open sea, are easily attainable.

The low, receding shores of Strangford Lough, with its multitude of tiny islands and occasional ruins of fine old castles, will suit those who wish for more peaceful seascapes. A few days might also be spent at Downpatrick, with its great rath, whose banks are a favourable point of view from which to sketch the lazy windings of the Quoile river, with a wooded middle distance; and yet further off, the first view of the lovely Mourne Mountains. Lovers of rougher sea and fishing boats will prefer to select Ardglass or Killough.

Passing on towards Newcastle we come to Dundrum, with a finely placed ruined castle and acres of sandhills gay with wild-flowers, making glorious foregrounds for the Mourne Mountains in one direction, or for the tumbling waters of the open sea in another.

From Newcastle, we pass along the coast road, with the Irish Sea on the left hand and the mountains on the right, seamed by noble valleys running into the heart of the range, beautiful with streams and tarns and heather and grey granite boulders. The little town of Kilkeel makes a capital sketching centre, offering great variety of scenery. Visitors should on no account leave Kilkeel without seeing the beautiful and very paintable Happy Valley, and obtaining permission to visit Lord Kilmorey's picturesque demesne of Mourne Park.

This scrapbook, then, is meant as a celebration of the quaint landscapes, both geographical and human, of 'the aul' County Down'. In the fading glass of the picture-postcard we see preserved those leisured, lazy days, not really so long ago, while verses by local bards, some long forgotten, and cuttings from newspapers and journals of the time help to invoke the curious magic of an era all too rapidly receding.

L. P. Hartley has said, 'The past is a foreign country. They do things differently there.' Perhaps. And yet, looking about, so much, thankfully, remains.

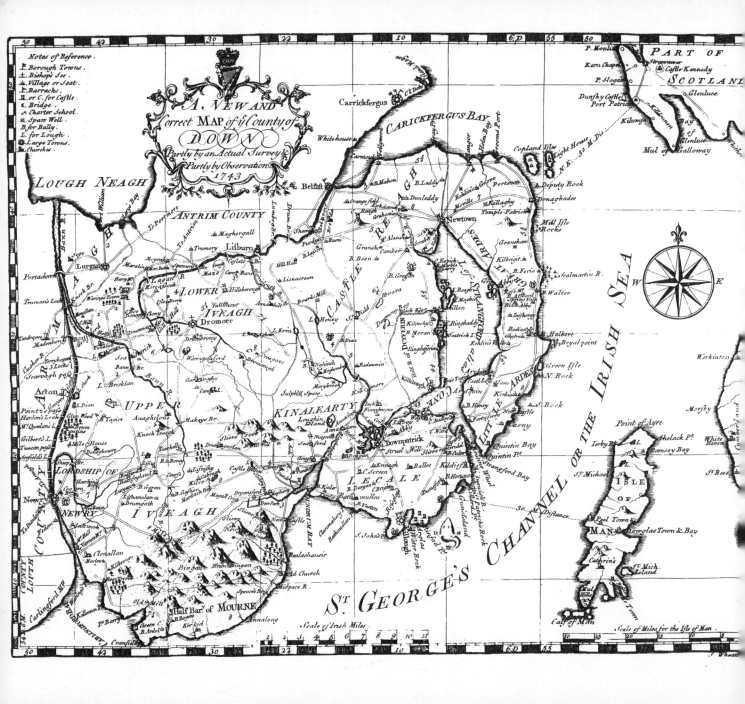

County Down

The Windin' Roads O' Down

I work my days in city streets
 Where bustlin' men wheek by,
All bent on gold they're grubbin',
 On each face a grim set frown;
But all the gold I long tae see
 Is gold beams from the sky,
Gold sunlight, on the highroads,
An' hawthorn-fragrant byroads,
 That wind thro' County Down.

I love the roads thro' Ball'nafeigh,
 An' Saintfield, an' Crossgar,
Ball'nahinch, an' Loughinisland
 Tae Mourne o' wide renown;
Or Strangford's road to bless Mahee,
 Where holy saint's bones are,
Not far-off from the highroads,
An' new-mown hay lined byroads,
 That wind thro' County Down.

I've seen grand highways in the States
 Frae East tae Middle-West—
When buds were breakin' intae leaf
 Or leaves were turnin' brown—
Great roads thro' France an' Italy,
 But still I love the best
The turnin', twistin' highroads,
An' cottage bordered byroads,
 That wind thro' County Down.

An', ere I die, mayhap, again
 I'll tramp strange roads afar—
Thro' old historic cities
 Bright wi' beauty's golden crown—
But ever will my heart hark back
 Tae where God's evenin' star
Beams down upon the highroads,
The wild rose scented byroads,
 That wind thro' County Down.

Padraic Gregory, *Complete collected Ulster ballads* (Belfast, 1959)

1

Old Bridge, Rostrevor.

Holywood

Annual Excursion

The morning dawned beautifully fine, the sea was like a veritable mill pond, and the prognostications were all of an optimistic turn. Everybody was smiling, and the goodly number of excursionists — some 500 — were in the best of spirits. Punctual to time, 8.15 a.m., the good ship "Vulture" slipped her cables at the quay, and we were off. The scene even at this hour down the harbour was an animated one. The numerous coal steamers hurry-scurrying with their disloading derricks, the rattling and hammering at the Queen's Island Shipbuilding yard went to convince one of the great hive of industry which has won for Belfast world-wide fame, the leviathans for the White Star Line were growing on the stocks like living things. The scene on the cross-Channel steamers was equally interesting. The decks were being scrubbed and made spec and span for the next voyage across the Channel. One found something interesting at every yard of the journey down the river, the Alexandra Dock fast reaching completion, and the busy throng of men removing one of the twin islands to make room for the onward stride of progress. On reaching the Lough proper a gentle breeze from the north was most enjoyable. The Bangor boat passing on our port side with its "early birds" for the city, who gave us a hearty cheer to speed us on our way. Holywood on our starboard is sending up its puffs of smoke showing that the inhabitants are at last getting about. The scenery on both sides of the Lough is very fine, and is much enjoyed. There was much to explore on the ship, some of our lady friends getting as far down as the stoke hold; others were interested in the engine room; while others paced the decks keeping a sharp look out for sea serpents or other such monsters. The Scotch coast was clearly in view from Blackhead, and Campbeltown was reached at shortly after 12 o'clock...

High St. (Holywood) Presbyterian Church Congregational & Guild Magazine, 1910

Holywood

These promenades are naturally the main resort of those who come to inhale health from the pure sea breezes; and furnish an unfailing resource for the lounger. At such hours as are usually devoted to out-door exercises, especially towards evening, when many, whose delicate constitution will not enable them to sustain the heat of the day, come forth to be invigorated by the saline breezes, it presents a pleasing and animated spectacle. During the time that the water is on the beach, which is about three hours in every tide, the gentle plashing of the waves upon the shingle within a few yards of promenaders' feet, induces that pensive and pleasing mood which poets describe.   * * *

Among the sources of amusement of the frequenter of the beach must not be omitted the numerous water parties, which in fine weather, especially towards the close of day, add greatly to the gaiety and interest of the scene, even to those who are too timorous or too bilious to venture on themselves; while, to the visitor who himself knows how to handle the oars, a high tide, a glass-smooth sea, and a setting sun, are irresistible attractions. A leap into one of the tight little crafts that float invitingly moored at the water's edge, and a silent sweep of his oar, soon sends him skimming over the mirror-like surface; which, for about an hour before sun-set in summer and autumn, reflects all the rich tints of the western sky.

Thomas T. Kelly, *A history of Holywood; the advantages which it affords as a summer retreat* (Belfast, 1850)

The town of Holywood, on the shores of the fine Lough of Belfast, is prettily situated. Commanding the most pleasing views and possessing so many advantages, it is surprising to find the requirements of sea-bathing left entirely out of the question. Several stationary private sheds are placed along the shore, and there is also a general shed and a long gangway out into the lough for men to avail themselves of. To see naked men running along these planks and groups on the rocks watching them, is amusing though not altogether civilized. Complaints are often made by the men-bathers of people looking on. How on earth either at Holywood or Bangor this can be helped under the present crude arrangements does not appear. In France and along the shores of the Mediterranean the men as well as the women wear a bathing-dress. We have much to learn in this country.

Irish Builder, 15 July 1867

Lough View Cafe.

HOLYWOOD.

Lough View Cafe (view taken from Grounds).

Holywood

A County Down Lyric

Holywood town
Comes back to me:
Though old I've grown,
My memory
Glides down the years;
And once again—
Eyes without tears,
Heart without stain,
All innocence,
I feel once more
The influence
Of hill and shore.
I'm four again,
And all is plain.
Come down this hill;
You'll see a rill
Crossing the lane;
And there again
Kissing Bridge stands.
Let's clap our hands!
Come on with me
And you shall see
An ancient wall—
For you that's all—
But once a snail
With horns and tail
And sparkling shell
Was there as well.
And so for me
With memory
That wall is full
And wonderful...

Herbert Moore Pim, *Songs from an Ulster valley* (London, 1920)

Clandeboye, Co. Down

Clandeboye

On a little monument, which stands in an obscure but beautiful and romantic spot in Lord Dufferin's demesne at Clannaboye (Clandeboye), and which bears the following inscription, now scarcely decipherable:— 'In memory of a loved and lamented nephew, Robert Temple Blackwood, who fell at the Battle of Waterloo, on Sunday, the 18th of June, 1815, this urn is placed here by Anna Dorothea Dufferin.'

Near where the limpid lake lies, clear and still,
Beneath the shelter of the tower-topped hill,
Reflecting back the glories of the west
As nature shuts her eye and sinks to rest;
Or smiling welcome to the cheering dawn
Which wakes again to life the graceful swan
And countless song-birds to their hymns of joy
Among the sylvan shades of Clannaboye:

Where deeper fall the shadows from the trees,
And brake and bramble bow before the breeze;
Lonely, sequestered, hid from prying eyes,
Save those that nightly twinkle from the skies;
Far from the beaten track where mortals tread;
In mem'ry of the long-lamented dead
There stands an urn, reared by a loving hand,
To him who, in a hostile, foreign land,
Served king and country gallantly and well,
Fought like a hero, like a hero fell;
And, dying, sprinkled with a gory dew
The fierce contested field of Waterloo!

Let others tell the deeds of Greece and Rome;
Raise high the statue; write the pond'rous tome;
Void of the benediction of a heart
'Tis mockery, all the pomp of wealth and art;
Let's judge them by the spirit which gave them
*   birth—*

The moving motive—not th' intrinsic worth:
Compared with them this humble piece of stone,
Standing perhaps forgotten or unknown;
Wet with the burning tears of queenly eyes;
Set by a heart, and chiselled by its sighs;
Though neither gold, elaborate, nor tall,
In sterling worth stands far above them all!

Sleep on, brave warrior, take thy well-earned rest;
Soft sigh the grass o'er thy once gallant breast;
Though she be dead who shed for thee her tears,°
And thou oblivious art to passing years;
Though "Earth to earth, and dust to dust" has
*   passed,*
Thy mem'ry, by this urn, will ever last;
But if the march of Ruin and Decay
Should tread it down, and it should pass away,
High on the deathless scroll of Britian's fame,
With Britain's noble son,* is carved thy name,
Where it shall stand while beats a heart that's true
To Britain or the fame of Waterloo!!

° The late Lady Dufferin, who erected the urn.
* The Duke of Wellington.

James H. Cousins, *Ben Madighan and other poems* (Belfast, 1895)

Helen's Tower

Lord Dufferin

Coming upon it suddenly in the midst of the billowing verdure of Clande-boye Demesne, you are lifted far beyond the low, dense levels of mere Success, into that rare atmosphere wherein mother love and son's devotion fuse in a golden silence. No servility, no flattery, no vainglory here; only the quiet and sincere assertion of the supremacy of the primal affections over all the equivocal honours the world can confer. Few men have been the recipient of so many distinctions as Lord Dufferin; fewer earned them so nobly; yet this' man who has been Governor-General of Canada, Viceroy of India, Ambassador at St. Petersburg and Constantinople, diplomatist, statesman, orator, explorer of those northern snows whose lonely beauty he has rendered in immortal prose, can return in the end to Clandeboye, all his honours forgotten in the thought of her whose teaching and example had been the inspiration of his career. As he walks through the upper chamber of the Tower, stopping for the thousandth time before the lines addressed to him when life was in its noon, the years of wise achievement fall from him, till he hears once more the words 'of the sweetest, most beautiful, most accomplished, wittiest, most loving and lovable human being that ever walked upon the earth.' No wonder the great Victorian poets vied with one another in musicked homage to the mute symbolism of this Tower raised by a chivalrous son in honour of a woman whose deep heart was known to him alone, but whose genius belongs to universal Poetry by virtue of 'The Irish Emigrant' and 'Terence's Farewell', lyrics of the homely human emotions which Burns would have loved.

Hugh A. MacCartan, *The glamour of Belfast* (Dublin, 1921)

Helen's Tower

Poems inscribed on brass plaques set on the walls of the boudoir in Helen's Tower.

On life's imperishable strand
  The tides of passion rage in vain;
With pearls of song they sow the sand,
  And this is our immortal gain.

So shall this love-enchanted Tower
  Win music from the waves of Time—
Transfigured into Helen's bower,
Till every stone shall ring with rhyme.

Lord Houghton, 24 May 1865

Helen's Tower here I stand,
Dominant over sea and land.
Son's love built me, and I hold
Mother's love in lettered gold.
Would my granite girth were strong
As either love, to last as long.
I should wear my crown entire
To and thro' the Doomsday fire,
And be found of angel eyes
In earth's recurring Paradise.

Alfred, Lord Tennyson (1861)

HELEN'S TOWER, CO. DOWN.   26312

Helen's Tower

Who hears of Helen's Tower may dream, perchance,
How the great beauty from the Scaean Gate
Gazed on old friends, unanimous in hate,
Death-doom'd because of her fair countenance.
Hearts would leap otherwise at thy advance,
Lady to whom this tower is consecrate,
Like hers, thy face once made all eyes elate;

Yet unlike hers, was bless'd by every glance.
The tower of hate is outworn, far and strange,
A transitory shame of long ago;
It dies into the sand from which it sprang,
But thine, love's rock-built tower, shall fear no change,
God's self laid stable earth's foundation so,
When all the morning stars together sang.

Robert Browning, 26 April 1870

12

THE STATION, HELEN'S BAY.

A Panoramic View at the Shore, Helen's Bay.

Bangor.

Colonel Sharman Crawford's

Photo 31243A4, Coon, Moira.

15

Crawfordsburn

This Ulster House once sold
Smuggler's Wine

The Old Inn at Crawfordsburn

The ripening wheat is gilding the fields along the highway that leads through Crawfordsburn from Holywood Priory to the ruins of Bangor's ancient Abbey. How many and how different the feet that have trodden this old road in the last fifteen hundred years.

The sandalled feet of pilgrims and monks and scholars, journeying between Bangor and Armagh; the cross-thonged feet of the Danes who desolated Abbey and town; the leather shod feet of the settlers, wary of the wolves that lurked thereabouts, the marching feet of Count Schomberg's army on the route from Ballyholme to the Long Bridge at Belfast — do any of these footsteps echo eerily about the gilded fields?

From the time that man left his caves, outgrew his liking for wood, and began to journey from place to place, there have been inns along the roads he travelled.

Certainly there has been an inn at Crawfordsburn since the hamlet took its name from those Scottish Crawfords who were tenants of Sir James Hamilton in the time of James I.

Striking feature

To-day the Old Inn is the most striking feature of the old road, its white and black standing sharp against the blues and greens and gold of the landscape.

That part of the dwelling which has been standing since 1614 is still thatched, and the musicians' gallery within serves to remind us of a time when the inn was the meeting place not only of peasant and yeoman, but of the lesser gentry who came, of an evening, to sample the foreign wines provided by mine host'

Piquancy

In this particular inn some of these foreign wines may have had the added piquancy of having evaded the Customs' officers for a former owner discovered secret hiding places used by smugglers. There was considerable smuggling between the Down coast and the Isle of Man right to the end of the eighteenth century.

The Ardglass peasant-poet, Burdy, tells us, in verse, that the free-traders took out meal, fruit, flax, whisky, flour, and potatoes, and returned with sugar, coffee, wine and rum.

The name of the hostelry must at one time have been 'The Old Ship Inn'. When I wonder, was the sign of the ship disregarded?

After the Hamiltons, the Montgomerys and the Stewarts had planted this part of Ulster, the Old Inn became a stopping place for the mail coach making connections with the sailing packets at Donaghadee. Here the horses were changed and many of the famous travellers to Ireland must have rested, at least for refreshment — certainly the Duke of Wellington was once a guest, and rumour has it that Peter the Great called when he made a visit to Ulster to study the manufacture of damask linen.

So many foreign coins were changed hereabouts in the seventeenth and eighteenth centuries that there was an accepted rate for the 'broad pieces' as the local inhabitants termed the pistoles and moidores.

Nowadays, although the mail-coach has given way to the touring-car, the broad-piece to the prosaic pound-note, there is still music in the gallery of the Old Inn as the fiddles play gaily to the wedding-guests, in the way they have almost "since Adam delv'd and Eve span."

Belfast Telegraph, 5 August 1953

Tea Room,
Crawfordsburn Inn.

Bangor

Of all the favoured spots on earth,
  Can aught compare with Bangor?
The very name inspires with mirth,
  And chases city languor.

To say you know not Bangor town,
  Or Ballyholme so charming,
Would dub you straight a backward clown
  Of ignorance alarming.

But since I find 'tis hard to rhyme,
  I'll hie me to the 'Pickie',
Where, 'mid a scene of bliss divine,
  Sport 'Knuts' and 'Flappers' tricky.

The fairest spot on all the land,
  A fitting frame for beauty,
Where youth and health go hand in hand,
  And joy the only duty.

The rippling waters waving beat
  Around each rock and crannie,
Where maids may find a cosy seat,
  And there dispense with 'Granny'.

* * *

Of Bangor fair, what need for rhyming,
  With rustic scenes and changing sea,
The scent of flowers thy footsteps guiding
  To sweet, romantic Carnalea.

The waters blue with sails are smiling,
  The mind in calm contentment strays;
The farther shore the thought beguiling
  Stores up a scene for future days.

But, bless my soul, I've sat here dreaming,
  And I must leave this haven bright.
Is it two weeks? Like days it's seeming.
  Farewell! thou dear old, gay fortnight.

M. Cleland, *Shine and shade* (Belfast, 193?)

Pickie Walk, Bangor, Co. Down.

Bangor

Report of the Medical Officer of Health

I find that hardly a case of infectious disease has its origin in the town. The sanitary arrangements and water supply are excellent. The entire town is kept remarkably clean. The hilly character of the district causes rapid surface drainage, and this, in conjunction with the very low rainfall, results in the streets drying very quickly. In summer the streets are watered from a motor watering cart with salt water, and consequently a beautiful road surface is obtained, free from dust. The air is dry, rarefied, bracing, and peculiarly exhilarating. This causes freer and more vigorous circulation, and the tissue change and elimination to be more active and rapid. A welcome feature to residents is the cooler temperature in the summer as compared with the cities and even the adjoining country, whilst in winter a low temperature has not the unpleasant characteristics of damper districts, the dry atmosphere making the keenest frosts enjoyable and bracing. The configuration of the town permits of the free ventilation of even the most sheltered parts, and the importance of this in preventing stagnation of the air accounts for the mortality returns being extraordinarily low, notwithstanding the fact that many invalids are sent to Bangor. Cases of enteric are almost unknown, and this is, no doubt, largely due to the first-class water supply and perfect sanitary conditions.

JOHN F. MITCHELL,
Medical Officer of Health

Nature, aided by Art, has made Bangor one of the most beautiful and healthy towns in Ireland, its average death rate being only 9.9.

Official guide to Bangor (Bangor, 1910?)

Bangor's present prosperity and its prospects for the future are mainly due to its delightful situation, together with its proximity to the City of Belfast. For the city's masses and the city's classes alike it forms a pleasant outlet from early spring till late autumn, and during "the season" its bracing air and its good bathing facilities — not to mention its picturesque surroundings — are fully taken advantage of. Of recent years, owing largely to the good train service, many citizens of Belfast have found it desirable to reside permanently in this healthful town, and indeed it might be mentioned that it is quite as convenient for them to do so as to live in some parts of the out-lying suburbs of the city; while the advantages of spending even the hours of slumber in the fresh sea air are too many and obvious to be enumerated here.

The new saloon paddle steamer, "Erin's Isle" — a vessel belonging to the Belfast and County Down Railway Company — conveys large numbers of passengers to and from the city during the months of summer, and this in itself is a boon much appreciated not only by daily travellers, but also by many thousands of workers of the poorer class, whose means do not permit of their spending a longer period than a few hours away from the scenes of their labour.

The Herald Almanac and County Down Directory (Bangor, 1915)

Bangor

Bangor On The Sea

Once at Bangor on the sea
  Stood I at the dawn of day,
Watched the first faint rays of morning
  Glimmering thro' the mist so gray;
Saw the far wave brighter glisten,
  Saw the white sails flutter free,
As the purple dawn was breaking
  There at Bangor on the sea.

Once at Bangor in the noontide,
  With the ocean at my feet,
Far I scanned its trembling bosom,
  Heard its mighty pulses beat;
Watched the white bird skim the waters,
  Felt the fresh breeze stirring free,
In the glorious noontide basking,
  There at Bangor on the sea.

Once at Bangor, when the sunset
  Streamed upon the glist'ning strand,
Flung a tinting—mystic—matchless,
  On the ocean and the land;
Walked I in the evening's quiet,
  Heard the ripple of the tide,
One that I had loved and longed for
  Came and lingered by my side.

Talked we of the ocean's vastness,
  And the beauty of the skies,
Talked of life that's short and strenuous,
  And of love that never dies,
Till the twilight paled and faded,
  And the wave gleamed bright no more,
And the darkness, swift descending,
  Muffled cliff, and sea, and shore.

Something brighter than the radiance,
  Wrapped about the fiery west—
Brighter far than sunset's glory,
  E'er did land and wave invest,
Broke upon our inward vision,
  Set our longing hearts aglow,
'Twas the fire of hope up-springing,
  Which before had moulder'd low.

'Twas the vision of the future,
  Showing all that life might be,
Breaking on our raptured spirits
  There at Bangor on the sea.

J.G. Thomson, *The breath of meadow hay* (Belfast, 1913)

Queen's Parade, Bangor

Bangor

There are the remains of twenty-five forts and raths in the parish, but the largest is at Rath-Gael. It covers two acres, and is surrounded by a double vallum. The first body of English forces under the Duke of Schomberg anchored in Groomsport Bay with 10,000 men, a small fishing village near Bangor which was formerly called "Graham's Port". King William afterwards created the Duke "Earl of Bangor", but he will always be known as Schomberg. It seems difficult to believe the Bangor of the olden time that suffered such severe disaster through plunder, fire and invasion can be the pleasant smiling place we are now familiar with.

Almost every general shop shows festoons of sand shoes, cascades of little buckets and bunches of wooden spades to delight the heart of the young Belfastians. The small builders design some wondrous architecture on the sandy beach, while the older generation disport themselves in the blue waters of the bay.

Long may Bangor flourish as a health-giving outlet for the city of Belfast.

Mary Lowry, *The story of Belfast and its surroundings* (London, 1916)

Ballymagee Street, Bangor.

Donaghadee

A Wisp Of Dulse

Accept this wisp of dulse, old pal,
  Sent you from o'er the sea,
From the shores of dear old Ulster,
  To remind you of the 'Dee.
I plucked them off the rocks one morn
  Down at the North Pier end,
And as they're still unrationed, George,
  I'm free them you to send.
If any of the boys are there,
  Pass each of them a share;
For neither sloak or Carrageen moss
  Can with rock dulse compare.
For dulse contains much iodine,
  More nourishing by far
Than any patent medicine
  Dispensed in pill or jar.
Craigavon spoke of 'tattie' cake,
  Admittedly rich and rare,
Producing rose-pink-white skin
  On colleen sweet and fair.
But don't forget that iodine
  Abounds in Ulster dulse,
And medicoes have certified
  It regulates the pulse.
Then munch and crunch and cut them fine,
  Those blades so salt and crisp;
There's nothing that your molars grind
  Will make you step so brisk.
The Yanks may think you're chewing gum,
  But you can let them see
The few salt-smelling nut-brown blades
  That grew in Donaghadee.

John Moore, cited by Michael McCaughan in his 'John Moore,
  a Donaghadee poet', *Irish Booklore*, vol 1, 1971

Donaghadee

The Port

t stands serene in sun or shade,
With semi-circle of Parade,—
With scented peat and fragrant smoke:—
And sturdy, quiet fisher-folk.

It's gay in flaunt of summer crowd,
While joyous children laugh aloud:
What whirl of life and holiday,
And pleasure-boats upon the bay!

But yet, I think, for those who dwell
Year in, year out, more potent spell
Is wov'n in winter, when the fine,
Keen breezes stimulate like wine—

When quiet of October days
Falls on the nigh-deserted ways,
Or when the night's bejewelled arch
Looks down amid the winds of March.

And sometimes when I wander far,
To places that much grander are,
Despite the wondrous sights I see,
Thoughts of the Port return to me,

And memories of the place arise—
Of homely sights to greet my eyes:—
The Moat, in sheen of sunset rain,
And motors racing from the train!

W.H.F. [Patterson], *Songs of a port* (Belfast, 1920)

Donaghadee, Co. Down.

RELIABLE SERIES.

Ballywalter

Lines On Ballywalter, Co Down

A clean little town on the board of the sea,
  It is Ballywalter they call it by namè,
It's the fairest in all my walks that I see,
  A sweet gem of joy on the rim of the main.

Its churches, its schools, its houses and halls,
  Comparing with others it easy outshines,
With its rocks and its shores, its burns and its falls,
  And bickering waters along through ravines.

With its boats and its flagstaff, its coastguards and
    quay,
  With glory and lustre commercial in view,
The marine passing by may glass from the sea
  His beacon and guide o'er the waters so blue.

The ground and the castle surpasses by far
  In its walks and its trees and verdure so green,
With nothing unpleasant their beauties to mar,
  All shining in glory, a picture supreme.

The lord of the mansion, with bountiful hand,
  The keystone who binds and holds all together,
The largest employer, with houses and land;
  The highest in rank, in wisdom, and siller.

The warrens with the brackens and pure sandy bays.
  The ships of commerce that are always in motion,
The long rock, Skullmartin, the lightship and waves,
  With old Scottish Isle on the brim of the ocean.

You may travel the South, the East and the West,
  Nor can you find beauties with these to compare;
When here all alone you are lull'd into rest
  By the songs of the birds and soft balmy air.

Adjoining the town is the home of the dead,
  With its verdure so green and young trees in
    bloom;
Its walks and its flowers and each grassy bed,
  Enrobing our friends we have laid in the tomb.

The poor and the wealthy, the lord of the soil,
  All our friends who are gone departed and blest,
From the pains of this life all its cares and its toil,
  They slumber together, they slumber in rest.

John Gaw, *Original poems* (Belfast?, 1899)

Well Road, Ballywalter.   *4408.*

Cloughey

Cloughey Bay

I see them in the hissing spume,
   I see them in the spray,
The ghosts of all the sailormen
   That sleep in Cloughey Bay.
(The rocks are white with spindrift
   And the wind is East today).

Ghosts of tall and gallant Dons,
   Bearded men of Spain,
That drove their stately galleons
   Across the Spanish Main,
But they will sail the seas no more
   Nor sing their songs again.

Dutchmen from the Zuyder Zee,
   Stolid men and slow,
That sailed with over-confidence
   A coast they didn't know,
And now their bones are bleaching white
   Among the rocks below.

Men from Greenock clipper-ships,
   That knew the Austral breeze,
Laughing men from Genoa
   And swarthy Portuguese,
Every sort of sailorman
   That sailed the Seven Seas.

Every kind of sailorman,
   That sailed upon the deep;
Cloughey Bay has claimed her share
   And holds them in her keep,
Till the lee-shore breakers roar,
   And wake them from their sleep.

The waves are swirling on the rocks,
   The wind is East today,
I hear a ghostly shanty-man
   Above the hissing spray.
And a ghostly chorus echoing—
O Lowlands far away,
O Lowlands, my Lowlands away.

John o' the North, *Various verses* (Belfast, 1945)

CLOUGHEY BAY.

Kirkistown

Kirk Castle

All hail thou ancient castled keep!
  Proud relic of a former day,
Thy ruined bastions, broad and deep,
  Now clothed in panoply of gray
  To me unerringly portray
The greatness that adorns thy fame,
  And fain would I devoutly pay
Due reverence to thy honoured name.

* * *

Dread echoes flit across the hall
  Where once the minstrel raised his song,
And I can fancy on thy wall,
  The spirits of the great and strong
  Stand, while I musing move along
The narrow, broken, tottering stair,
  Which gallants in their day did throng
With many a lord and lady fair.

* * *

Thou standest here beside the wave,
  As stands an aged man beside
The ancient, solitary grave,
  Where all the friends of youth abide:
  Time's boisterous overwhelming tide
Has spared thee for a little space;
  But those on whom thou didst confide
Have fled thee—for another place.

Dominick Dunwoodie, *Poetical scraps and sketches*
(Belfast, 1842)

Kirkistone Castle, formerly the seat of the Savages of Kirkistone.

QUINTON CASTLE, PORTAFERRY.

Portaferry

Sweet Portaferry

You may gaze from green mountains across the bright seas, Where
wonder and pleasement are tak--ing their ease. You may search the world
o--ver from there to Ja-pan, Trans-ported with nature and the
glory of man. But why should men toil foreign lands to ex-
plore, When wonder and pleasement are here at the door, And
who would go ro---ving thro' country and town, From
sweet Port-a---fer---ry and the Kingdom of Down.

It lies on a harbour convenient and free—
Where the waters of Strangford run swirling to sea
To bear on their bosom the yield of our toil,
When farmer and fisherman plough lake and soil;
There bright silver comes in our nets to the strand
Our gold and our glory are planted by hand;
But who would change beauty for gain or renown
And leave Portaferry and the Kingdom of Down?

O, if I were a poor man I'd work on my land
Content with the beauty of every hand;
But if I were a rich man my care to beguile
I'd fill up my pockets and wander awhile;
And what though I'd wander on strange lands and seas
And think my land middling compared against these—
I know when old age makes a sage of a clown
I'd seek Portaferry and the Kingdom of Down.

cited in Colm O Lochlainn's *More Irish Street Ballads* (Dublin, 1965)

Portaferry.   Co. Down.

Strangford Lough

ACCIDENT IN STRANGFORD LOUGH

Feared Loss Of A Mountstewart Boating Party
Eight Persons Missing

Our Newtownards correspondent, writing last night, says:— One of the most awful boating accidents which have occurred for years in the North of Ireland took place on Thursday afternoon or night in Strangford Lough, through which there is hardly a doubt eight persons have lost their lives. It would appear from all the facts we have been able to gather that on Thursday morning, before Lord and Lady Londonderry left for Belfast to open the exhibition, the marchioness, with her usually kindly disposition, gave permission to the servants of Mountstewart House to take her own boat for a sail on the lough. Some of them availed themselves of the offer, and the party comprised Mrs. Dougal, the housekeeper, who has been only about a fortnight at Mountstewart; Mrs. Taunt, the cook; Mr. Greinge, housesteward; Mr. Rowe, valet to Lord Londonderry; Mr. Start, valet to Lord Enniskillen; a young lady's maid to Lady Kathleen Cole, and two seamen named Hagan in Lady Londonderry's employment, who had charge of the boat. Mr. Rowe, it may be stated, is only about a month married. The party left Mountstewart boathouse, on the shores of the lough, about twelve o'clock, and they had provided themselves with lunch-baskets, intending, as is supposed, to lunch on one of the islands. The boat is a small open one, with sails. They sailed to Kircubbin, where they called, and left it about three o'clock in the afternoon. Nothing whatever has since been heard of them although every bay and village on the shores of the lough have been searched and examined. Portions of the lunch-baskets and sails have been discovered on an island near Portaferry, and the current at this spot is very strong. As we have said, up to the time of writing there is no trace of boat or occupants, and all hope has been given up. It is the general opinion that the boat was caught in one of the squalls which are very prevalent on the lough, and was swamped with all on board, leaving no one to tell the tale.

Belfast News-letter, 13 April 1895

Strangford Lough and Scrabo Hill, Newtownards.

697/73

Newtownards

Town's Survey

In a previous brief notice of this town we congratulated the inhabitants on its extremely cleanly aspect, and the freedom from mud and slush so observable in its streets; but it seems that since that period the householders have discovered that they were not liable to pay rates. They have literally "kicked against" contributing to corporate funds, and the consequence is, that the streets now remain unscavenged, and during a continuance of wet weather — such as has prevailed recently — one has to wade through mud, ankle deep. To the fairer portion of the town's people — the character of whose attire does not admit of their wearing the protecting "leggings" now so generally worn by "the lords of the creation" — this must prove most annoying, and indeed such a state of things is, to say the least, a great slur on the gallantry of the Newtonards gents. They have every right in other respects to be proud of their town; it is well laid out with spacious streets, and has a market square and market house, second to none in Ireland, and vastly superior to many with double its population, which is about 10,000 inhabitants. The commercial houses are numerous and well kept, evidencing a "very well to do" position of their owners in spite of the recent protracted depression of trade, owing to the American war. We learn with great pleasure that there is *now* constant employment for the poor of both sexes in weaving and spinning, although the average earnings are admittedly low, being about five shillings per week per adult. In many parts of the town the habitations of the poor are miserable and dirty, but not generally so bad as we have noticed elsewhere...

The outlets of Newtonards are much frequented for their pleasing scenery, and the excellent sea bathing afforded along the Carrickfergus shore.

Dublin Builder, 1st Dec. 1863

Old Cross, Newtownards

Downpatrick

At length I did arrive in ancient Down—
As fine a place as any to be found;
It to describe I will not take in hand:
But 'tis a handsome place as in our land.
The buildings there are mostly the first-rate,
In this fine County—'tis a town of state.
The chief it is, as many well do know,
Of County Down—we there do find it so.
It has a large Cathedral—nought compare
To it in all the Irish nation fair:
A Gaol quite new, upon a rising ground,
As strongly built as any to be found;
And near to it does stand a Danish Mount:
I'll soon give o'er in giving this account.
But the Infirmary I can't pass by,
A building fine—on it I cast my eye:
'Twas only there I took a distant view;
I then went on, my business to pursue.
Not far from Down, stands Hollymount, so grand,—
As beautiful a place as in the land.
It is adorned with woods and plantings there,
On a high ground, most pleasant, I declare:
I'll therefore, now, no longer persevere,
But finish the account I've given here.

William Anderson, *Original poems, sacred, moral,
elegaic, descriptive, misc.* (Belfast, 1841)

R.C. Pro. Cathedral, Downpatrick

Downpatrick

Ah, who will sing the glorious days of eld,
When all things flourished. When Downpatrick held
A leading place in commerce. When our fairs
Were thick-packed gatherings, interchanging wares.
Down was a town in old election times:
We paid our men for shouting—writing rhymes;
The good old days when each man boiled his pot,
And still had money, paying "scot and lot".
The night before the final polling-day,
Both sides sat up, preparing for the fray;
Cart loads of sticks were cut and smuggled in,
You might have seen them neatly piled in bin,
To be served out at early morning light—
(Oh, speak it low)—to rowdies hired to fight!

But few need now care how elections run,
Bereft of pay and all devoid of fun;
For me, I think I would not leave my seat
To give a vote, no matter who'd entreat.
The other day, when all Lecale was poll'd,
I never saw the colour of their gold.
I set myself to watch with all my might,
There was not even drink for thirsty wight.
Ah, how unlike the days of Keown and Ker,
When fortunes might be made at every bar;
When ale and porter flowed, and beeves were killed
Until each hungry maw was three times filled;
And crisp bank notes, too, fluttered here and there,
The poor man catching what the rich could spare.

J.W. Montgomery, *Fireside lyrics* (Downpatrick, 1887)

Market Street, Downpatrick.

English Street and Old Market Cross, Downpatrick

Ardglass

Far-famed Ardglass, thou town yclept "green height",
Thy castles sparkle in the full moon's light;
A fleet of boats surrounds thy shapely pier,
While, farther out, the white-maned horses rear,
And rush in fury on the iron shore,
Now breaking noiseless, now with deafening roar.
'Roll on, thou deep and dark blue ocean—roll';
Thy presence fills with awe the reverent soul.
Yet thou art not omnipotent—'twere wrong
To hold thee so: for here, though fresh and strong,
Yea, grand as when the great bard stroked thy name,
And poured upon thee his sublimest strain,
These stubborn rocks can intercept thy way,
And fling thee from them—ground to harmless spray.

Far-famed Ardglass, we know thy history all,
And lingering by each crumbling castle wall,
Our mind goes back to trace the misty past,
When war's loud trumpet brayed upon the blast
Recall the horrors of that darksome time,
When all thy cells were stained with hideous crime,
When ruthless chieftains ceaseless warfare waged
With brother chieftains, and wild passions raged,
Thy churches blazing in the dead of night,
Whilst all around lay universal blight.

*   *   *

Go on Ardglass, and prosper in thy ways,
The bard would crown thee with unfading bays;
Thy staple trade at times seems somewhat low,
But "mean" thou art not; for a cheering glow
Of right good nature shines along thy streets,
And at each turn the weary traveller greets;
Thy houses, too, are not mere "cabins"; fine
Substantial structures many a street-way line.
And in thy "Crescent" many a cosy nook
Attracts the wight who loves his pipe and book;
Here gentry, doctors, clergymen at ease,
Enjoy great leisure, living as they please,
And if thy dock were only neatly cleaned,
And all thy children from late night sprees weaned,
One scarce could find a town that would surpass
The many-castled seaport, famed Ardglass.

J.W. Montgomery, *Fireside lyrics* (Downpatrick, 1887)

Ardglass

This town of Ardglass, although in the reign of Queen Elizabeth one of the three principal towns in the county, next to Newry and Down, is now in a mean condition, consisting only of a few ordinary cabins, and four or five old decayed castles, besides a large ruined building, which will be mentioned hereafter. One of these castles, called the King's Castle, has been a large, strong building, near which are the ruins of a church; another, called Horn Castle, is only a plain building, yet of some strength for defence; a third is called the Coud Castle, but the natives could give no account of the meaning of the word, or the reason for the name.

* * *

We had like to have passed over Jordan's Castle, which, though not so large as the King's Castle, is yet handsomer than that or any of the former, and is a fort of considerable strength. It is memorable for the defence made hero by the valiant owner, Simon Jordan, who held it out three years in the Tyrone Rebellion, till he was relieved by the Lord Deputy Mountjoy, on the 17th of June, 1601.

* * *

The church of Ardboll was the ancient parish church of Ardglass, but was removed into the town (as tradition says) on account of its being desecrated by a cruel murder committed by the clans of the Macartanes on the whole congregation, at the Christmas midnight mass.

Harris's History of County Down, 1744

Ardglass

Little Boats

There go the little boats,
Out on the sea
To bring back the silver fish
For you and for me.
There go the little boats,
Come see them pass,
Out of the harbour mouth,
Out of Ardglass.

John Irvine, *By winding roads* (Belfast, 1950)

In Ardglass, Co. Down.

Newcastle

Whether we look to the extent and variety of its accommodation, the numbers that resort to it, its spacious open bay, and firm sloping sandy beach, or its magnificent scenery of mountain, wood, and water, Newcastle may be fairly termed the "Irish Scarborough, or Queen of Northern Bathing places". The advantages which it possesses have not been unappreciated, as is proved by the distance from which it attracts visitors in the summer months. It is situated on the bay of Dundrum, which is open to the eastward, having within a few years sprung up from a fishing hamlet to a cheerful and handsome little town, consisting of ranges of white houses, and vine-trellised cottages, lying in triple row along the base of Slieve Donard, which rises sheer over the level of the sea mark, to a height of nearly 2800 feet. Amongst the delightful environs of Newcastle, we may include the quiet English looking village of Bryansford, Dundrum, with its ivy-clad castle now in ruins, and the grand and picturesque scenery of Tullamore Park. The invalid whose case is likely to be benefitted by clear, pure, bracing sea and mountain air, can choose no more appropriate summer residence than this; whilst Donard Lodge and Tullamore Park open to strangers by the courtesy of their noble proprietors, afford an endless variety of interesting walks, rides and drives.

Newcastle abounds in every description of furnished lodgings, and houses may be had varying in price from ten shillings to five pounds per week. There is every convenience for the enjoyment of hot, cold, and shower baths, with an abundant supply of fish, and provisions of all kinds at a moderate rate. A very good light chalybeate water, which was brought under my notice through the politeness of Lady Annesley, is situated on the slope of Slieve Donard, which may be reached by a bracing walk, or by a carriage way newly constructed, when there is anything to deter from up hill walking. The great Mourne range of mountains, extending from this point to Dundrum bay, is a magnificent rampart, Slieve Donard being the highest of the chain. The axis of this range, to use the description of Scouler, is granite, flanked by masses of greenstone, hornblende, and schists, the primary formations being succeeded by greywacke schists. It contains more hornblende than the Wicklow granite, and is marked by the reddish colour of its felspar in place of the pearly white which characterizes the former. Fine crystals of topaz, beryl, emerald, and amethyst, are occasionally found in the hills and mountain rivulets.

Alexander Knox, *The Irish watering-places, their climate, scenery and accommodations* (Dublin, 1845)

NEWCASTLE, CO. DOWN.   Copyright.

Newcastle

Apart entirely from the natural beauty of Newcastle, its situation in the very centre of a district rich in objects both of antiquarian and historic interest imparts an interest to which few if any tourists are insensible. It is, in short, a watering-place possessing charms for every class of visitor. Reflecting on the many splendid ruins, the still glens, the lofty mountains, and majestic waterfalls, which are so plentiful in the surrounding district, one recalls De Quincey's fine account of Wordsworth's early home among the English lakes, and feels inclined to say of this resort as the great Opium Eater said so beautifully of the poet's home:— "The whole was one paradise of virgin beauty; the rare works of man all over the land were hoar with the grey tint of an antique picturesque; nothing was new, nothing was raw and uncisatrised."

* * *

But the great attraction to the Newcastle excursionist is the beautiful domain of Donard Lodge, which is open to visitors on every week-day. To realise the beauty of these grounds is impossible to one who has not visited and seen them under favourable circumstances, but the following brief description may be acceptable to the tourist:—

"The walks are laid out with great taste; flowering shrubs, rhododendron, arbutus, and fuschia grow luxuriantly, and blend pleasingly with firs, larches, and other trees. The principal feature, however, is the Glen River and its waterfalls. It rises in the deep glen between Slieve Donard and Slieve Commedagh, and rushes down the lowest part of its course in a succession of cataracts. None of these are very high; nor is the river wide; but the effect is always striking after heavy rains. One of these falls (at a spot called the Hermit's Glen, from a small cell artifically made under a huge rock) does not leap over a precipice, but slides, as it were, down a steep sloping rock, and is broken into two streams which unite at the base. As this rock stands obliquely to the course of the stream, the waterfall is presented *in profile* to one standing or sitting at a point of view below it. Near this fall is the Dining House, commanding an admirable view, and whence, if the day is clear, may be seen the tower of Down Cathedral, the monument to the Marquis of Londonderry, and Lough Strongford."

Belfast News-letter, 12th May 1890

SLIEVE DONARD HOTEL, NEWCASTLE, CO. DOWN

Newcastle

Sabbath Breaking
June, 1914

In the middle of June on a fine Sunday evening
I went for some pleasure to Newcastle strand,
But I still heard it said, Sunday pleasure was
    grieving,
But I meant for to go with a heart and a hand.

So I got in the train down at old Ballyroney
And she steered me right off till she stopped at
    the shore
When I walked on the platform and looked all
    around me
I soon found the pleasure wasn't worth an encore.

I joined some companions while I walked, I was
    thinking
That people at home are far better than there;
The pub's they were open and the men they were
    drinking
And leaving their homes wrecked, their wives
    in despair.

Then we sat on the wall and we looked at the
    ladies;
Some walked on the footpath and some sat on
    stools
I thought to myself we're no better than babies,
We are all a party of half-witted fools.

When it came near to train-time we got some
    refreshments
And into a tea-room we all sure did go:
We ordered some tea and meat cut to fragments
When we looked at the time sure our watches
    were slow.

Then we went to the street and we walked out
    with courage,
When we came to the station the train was away:
Said I "Police Barracks would do us for storage,
We deserve nothing better for breaking God's day."

Then I spoke to a carman—don't know what
    they called him;
He charged us five bob and just left us half home,
He bubbled and talked of horse riding and
    jumping;
Not a word of the Bible or his last harvest home.

Then we sighed and we said we have had great
    misfortune,
In breaking God's day when we went to the shore,
And all who do thus they will find disappointment,
They will have all the week their foul deeds to
    deplore.

Now all who seek pleasure go on Tuesday or Monday;
You will have better times and more money in
    store;
But to buy or to sell or to spree on a Sunday
Will leave empty pockets and loss to deplore.

William Rowan, *Poetical works* (Belfast, 1927)

Main Street and Post Office, Newcastle, Co. Down

Newcastle

Slieve Denard

Oh! have you climb'd the giddy steep
   Of Denard's mountain piles,
And view'd below the foaming deep,
   Extending many miles!

Loud thunders down the hoarse cascade,
   Through wild and rocky dells,
And roars conceal'd beneath the shade
   Of purple heather bells.

Huge crags are there of granite rock,
   And gray primeval stone;
With angles, rounded by the shock
   Of mouldering time alone.

And toward brown Denard's hoary top,
   Where thunder-tempest raves,
A hundred mountain heads look up,
   As tributary slaves.

And on that region wild and high,
   Enchanting to the view,
The lovely lake delights the eye,
   So aptly named the "Blue".

* * *

John Williamson, *Poems on various subjects* (Belfast, 1839)

"Where The Mountains of Mourne Go Down To The Sea."

Oh! Mountains of Mourne
majestic and high,
In dreams you come back to me,
With your mist crowned head
'neath the Irish sky,
An' the tip of your toe in the sea.
—Eva Brennan.

Kilkeel

Up In The Mountains

Up in the mountains
Lookin' on the sea,
If I was home again
It's there I'd be;
Far from this dark city's
Noisy loom an' wheel,
Up in the mountains
Above Kilkeel.

Och, when I left you
It's proud you were an' high,
Scorn on your red lip
An' anger in your eye,
An' little was I guessin'
The lonesome I'd feel,
Far from the mountains,
Far from Kilkeel.

Thrawn folk are lovers,
Foolish lad an' lass,
But won't your heart grow kind again
As the days pass?
Send the one word to me
I'll turn upon my heel
And seek you in the mountains
Above Kilkeel.

Richard Rowley, *County Down songs* (London, 1925)

60

THE HARBOUR, KILKEEL, Co. DOWN. 1969 W.L.

Rostrevor

Rosstrevor — Beautiful Rosstrevor, as the concurrent voice of all tourists pronounces it to be — is not only the abode of peace and loveliness, but is perhaps the most salubrious spot in the three kingdoms — the air being at once mild and bracing, and acting almost as a specific for more complaints than any one place mentioned in Dr. Grenville's 'Spas of Europe'. What would not thousands of dyspeptics, hypochondriacs, and invalids of all sorts, who now in vain seek health and tranquillity in the noisy, dirty, bustling, suburban-looking, and thrice cockneyfied Welsh and English watering-places, give to know of the existence of this little Elysium! It is as yet unpolluted by the stream of frowsty match-making dowagers, with antiquated daughters, intent only on husbandcide; and free of all the usual loungers, sharpers, and equivocals of both sexes, who make up the summer population of the average run of these localities.

A picturesque handbook to Carlingford Bay and the watering-places in its vicinity
(Belfast, 1846)

PROMENADE AND GREAT NORTHERN HOTEL, ROSTREVOR, CO. DOWN.

Rostrevor

A Picnic At Rostrevor

It lies 'twixt the sea and the mountain,
   Or rather the bay and the hill,
Which cool the warm breath of the summer,
   And take from the winter its chill.
It nestles 'mid oak-trees and beeches
   That stretch their green arms o'er the street,
Whose breadth, to its length nearly equal,
   Expands where the four roadways meet.
As you wind by the bay's breezy margin,
   Rostrevor you mark from afar,
Betrayed by its spire of Our Lady's,
   And joyful you cry: 'Here we are!'—
Betrayed by its spire gleaming brightly
   High o'er its embowering trees:
As the breath of the sea is detected
   In this bracing and life-giving breeze.
That white granite spire of Our Lady's
   On the oaks and the beeches looks down,
And it cries up to heaven for a blessing
   On the simple Arcadian town.
A blessing in sooth is the convent
   That hides in the shadow serene
Of that beautiful Church of our Lady,
   Of Mary our Mother and Queen.

The convent and church crown the village
   Which clusters in peace at their feet;
A stream from the hills saunters past it,
   Reluctant to leave scene so sweet.
Dark stream where the branches hang thickly,
   Bright stream where the sun pierces through;
'Tis shallow, yet keeps a broad channel—
   Who knows what the winter may do?
A bridge takes you over this river
   Which dreamily murmurs along,
Too lazy to wet all its pebbles,
   Too lazy for ripple or song.
You then, 'neath the long, leafy branches
   Interlacing o'erhead, wend your way,
Near plashing of waves on the shingle,
   Towards the mouth of the mountain-locked bay.
And soon on your left you will notice
   The Woodside Hotel at the quay—
(This rhyme is pronounced as if rhyming
   With not very distant Crock Shee,
Though personal taste would incline me
   To go for a rhyme to Mill Bay;
But Walker and Worcester and Webster
   Conspire to point t' other way.)

(cont'd)

R.C. Church Rostrevor Co. Down.

Further on, the road glides through a forest
  Which covers the mountain's steep side—
Green leaves all around you, above you,
  Down, down to the brink of the tide.
And here, where the Wood House lies hidden,
  A path tempts you up through the trees—
But first let me risk a suggestion
  You're free to' reject if you please.
This climbing of mountains is pleasant
  For lads loose from schoolroom and desk;
But a well-furnished hamper enhances
  The beauty of scenes picturesque.
Without a fat hamper ascend not!
  We're made of both body and soul;
Ev'n poets can't do without dinner,
  And maybe 'tis best on the whole.
So take turn about with the hamper,
  And, crawling zigzag, scale the steep;
Puff, pant, and perspire towards the summit,
  Disturbing the mountaineer sheep.
These, wiry and hardy and agile,
  Climb mountains more deftly than you
Who frequently find it expedient
  To pause and admire the view.

Come, rest in the shade of this boulder,
  Called truly in Irish Clough More,
Once hurled o'er the lough by the giant
  Who fought from the southern shore.
You see where the Carlingford giant
  Lies under yon mountain ridge high—
In outline his figure recumbent
  Is traced clear against the blue sky.
Here, too, you observe how his fingers
  Sank deep in this wonderful stone—
But now peradventure your hunger
  Sufficiently wolfish hath grown.
Clough More shall behold a new battle;
  Here pitch we our camp for a halt.
Be hampers unpacked! Where's the corkscrew?
  I fear we've forgotten the salt.
With eating and laughing and quaffing,
  Uncounted the sunny hours pass,
Where the bottles of many a picnic
  Are strewn o'er the crisp, trodden grass.

(cont'd)

Woodside Rostrevor Co. Down.

Rostrevor (cont'd)

Awaiting dessert, you have leisure
  To bend your rapt gaze on the scene—
These parallel ranges of mountain,
  The salt waves that sparkle between,
The white sails that speckle those waters,
  The cornfields that speckle the side
Of yon mountain, repulsing the heather
  Far up from the marge of the tide.
Where the mountains slope downward and inland,
  And melt in blue distance away,
The stout Frontier-town of old Newry
  Keeps guard at the head of the bay.
God bless the good town and each homestead
  That peoples this ocean-lake's shore,
All round from the Hill of the Violets
  To the lighthouse that faces Greenore!

In yonder must lie Narrow Water,
  Where smoke-wreaths from Warrenpoint town
Curl upward beyond this rich woodland
  Of green, patched with yellow and brown.
How white winds the road down beneath us!
  Ev'n dust at this distance looks nice!
'Tis well to commune thus with Nature—
  (Oh! thank you, just give me one slice.)

At last we hie homeward. The journey
  Down hill through the crags and the trees
(The freight of the hamper stowed elsewhere)
  Is made with comparative ease.
How swift, how unheeded the swiftness
  Of the last downhill stage of life's way!
How pleasant is home to the weary!
  In heav'n may we feel it one day!

But ah! though the charms I have chanted
  Have dear to my memory grown,
I think of thee more, O Rostrevor!
  Because thou art near to Killowen.

Rev. Matthew Russell, *Idyls of Killowen* (London, 1905)

Narrow Water Castle, Warrenpoint
Of very ancient origin. Erected to command passage of river. Destroyed
17th century, and rebuilt by Duke of Ormond.

Warrenpoint

To Warrenpoint I then did take my way,
And some few days I in that place did stay;
Most beautiful it is, to an extreme—
The fancy it does strike a pleasant theme.
The town is small, resembles a half moon,
Does nearly face the sun when it is noon.
On South-west side there is a famous quay,
Where there much shipping does come in, we see,
And many lighters there from that same quay,
To Newry town the goods they do convey.
'Tis just four miles, they say, from Newry town,
The utmost point it is of County Down:
I think to nearly Southward it does lie—
The County Louth across, 'tis very nigh;
Its situation is upon that bay
Of Carlingford, as now I here do say.
The bay these counties it does them divide,
Where rolling billows swell with force and pride.
Upon the Northern side of it does stand,
All on a level ground—fine fertile land.
The houses all are elegant and white—
On a fine Summer day you'd take delight
To view the place, adorn'd by Nature's hand,
And art combin'd, in that fine pleasant land.
In Summer season numbers do repair
Unto that place, for bathing do go there,
For recreation, benefit, likewise;—
Of health that's pure we greatly should it prize.

William Anderson, *Original poems, sacred, moral,*
elegaic, descriptive, misc. (Belfast, 1841)

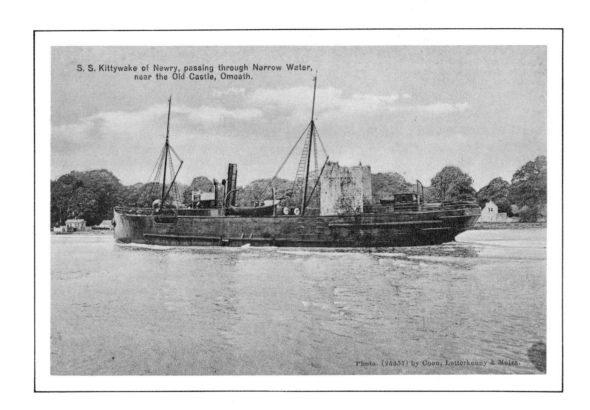

S. S. Kittywake of Newry, passing through Narrow Water,
near the Old Castle, Omeath.

Photo. (25357) by Coon, Letterkenny & Moira.

Newry

WHATEVER the witty Dean of Saint Patrick's may have said to the contrary, is well built, the streets remarkably clean, and the suburbs, in all directions, of great beauty. It is much changed since Swift immortalised it in a bitter couplet,—

"High church, low steeple,
Dirty street, and proud people."

Newry is fifty miles north of Dublin, thirty south-west of Belfast, and fifteen south-east of Armagh. It sits upon the Newry Water, but anciently known as the Clanrye, which, having in its course from Drumlough been enlarged by various influxing streams, is here a noble river, dividing the counties of Armagh and Down, and, mingling its waters with the tide at Newry, disemboguing itself five miles southward of the town into Carlingford Lough. Newry has great natural advantages of situation. It stands in the centre of the lovely valley through which the river flows from Carnmeen, on the margin of the most magnificent grouping of naturally picturesque landscape in Ireland. It is bounded by high hills on the east and west, those being again bounded, at a greater distance, by the mountains of Mourne on the east, among which is the pyramidal peak of Donard, the monarch mountain of Ireland and, overhanging the town on the west, are the Newry mountains, Tovnabane, and the still more distant and lofty Sliev Gullion. The country to the north, through which the canal, the river, and the great north road pass, is low and fertile, and ornamented with beautiful villas peeping out from among the trees, and white cottages surrounded with orchards and gardens. To the south, the scenery is more bold and wildly diversified; before you are rich meadow holmes and corn fields waving with luxuriant fertility; sheets of park scenery, emerald lawns, groves, and thickets of gigantic evergreens and primeval forest trees, surrounding Greenwood Park, Narrow Water House, Oriel House, Fathom Park, and Ashton; the hills and mountains on either side richly robed in the foliage of the forests; and closing the scene, the Alpine crest of Sliev Foy looking proudly down upon the combination of romantic beauty which pre-eminently distinguishes the scenery of Lough Carlingford.

A picturesque handbook to Carlingford Bay and the watering-places in its vicinity (Belfast, 1846)

Warrenpoint, Havelock Place, Co. Down.

Newry

During the course of 1842 our town received a visit from William M. Thackeray, who, in this year made a tour through a considerable portion of Ireland, and afterwards gave the world his impressions in his "Irish Sketch Book" under the *nom-de-plume* of Michael Angelo Titmarsh. Of Newry he speaks in the following terms:—

"Newry is remarkable as being the only town I have seen which has no cabin suburb; strange to say, the houses begin all at once, handsomely coated and hatted with stone and slate; and, if Dundalk was prosperous, Newry is better still. Such a sight of neatness and comfort is exceedingly welcome to an English traveller, who, moreover, finds himself, after driving through a plain, bustling, clean street, landed at a large, plain, comfortable inn, where business seems to be done, where there are smart waiters to receive him, and a comfortable warm coffee room that bears no traces of dilapidation ...

"Steamers to Liverpool and Glasgow sail continually. There are mills, foundries, and manufactories, of which the guide book will give particulars; and the town, of 18,000 inhabitants, is the busiest and most thriving that I have yet seen in Ireland...

"Newry has many comfortable and handsome public buildings; the streets have a business-like look, the shops and people are not too poor, and the southern grandiloquence is not shown here in the shape of fine words for small wares. Even the beggars are not so numerous, I fancy, or so coaxing and wheedling in their talk. Perhaps, too, among the gentry, the same moral change may be remarked; and they seem more downright and plain in their manner; but one must not pretend to speak of national characteristics, from such a small experience as a couple of evenings' intercourse may give."

Newriensis, *A historical sketch of Newry* (1876)

TREVOR HILL, NEWRY.

Newry

The Jolly Sailor-Man

One day I went through Newry,
In a pub beside the Quay,
I met a jolly sailor-man,
Good-day, sez he till me.
Good-day yerself, sez I till him,
An' will ye take a dram?
I'll not say no, sez the sailor,
For it's drouthy that I am.

Then him an' me had pints apiece,
An' he began to tell
Tales of his voyage roun' the world,
An' all that there befell.
But thon porter had a head on it
Richer nor any crame,
I'll not say no, sez the sailor,
Till another o' the same.

I can't understand, sez he till me,
Why young chaps stays ashore.
When seamen travels aroun' the world,
Pickin' up gold galore,
For an inland life is a weemin's life
But at sea is a life for men,
An' I'll not say no, sez the sailor,
If ye wet my whistle again.

So he set his lip to the third good pint,
An' I paid the whole half-dozen;
Sez he, I know an Admiral,
An' him my mother's cousin.
I'm thinkin' o' joinin' the navy,
For he'll give me a high command,
An' I'll not say no, sez the sailor—
Sez I, it's your turn to stand.

Wi' that he ups an' squares at me,
Till he seen I was twice his size;
Then out he flung, an' slammed the door,
Wi' murder in his eyes.
Now I'm not mane, an' I'll buy a drink
For a friend has got a thirst,
But when next I meet a sailor-man,
I'll wait till he asks me first.

Richard Rowley, *Ballads of Mourne* (Dundalk, 1949)

Hill Street, Newry

Hilltown

Hilltown

There's a wee town,
In South Down,
Near Mullaghmore;
Where the goats wander
And the cattle dander
At your door.

There's turf smoke,
And there's kind folk
By the fires,
And the lark sings
Where the corn springs,
An' never tires.

On each spray
By the roadway
Sits a yella-yite,
An' the bees bum
An' the clegs come,
An' bite.

An' the trout rise
At the little flies
By the stream.
An' you lay your head
On a heather bed
An' dream.

An' you eat a heap,
An' you breathe deep
On the hills;
An' you find a cure
For most of your
Ills.

I'll away down
To Hilltown
When I can
Over yonder,
Where the goats wander,
By the Bann.

Rosamund Praeger, *Old-fashioned verses and sketches* (Dundalk, 1947)

Downshire Arms Hotel, Hilltown, Co. Down.

Castlewellan

On Slieve-Na-Man

If I was in Castlewellan
I'd have the fun o' the fair,
But up on Slieve-na-man,
Och! It's lonely there.
Only the clouds an' the hills,
An' a scoldin' mother to sort me;
If I was in Castlewellan
I'd have a young fellow to court me.

If I was in Castlewellan
I'd buy bright ribbons to wear,
With high-heeled shoes on my feet,
An' a Spanish comb in my hair.
But up on Slieve-na-man
There's work I must bend my back to,
Pigs an' cattle to feed,
An' never a boy to crack to.

Up on the mountain-side
There's only the whin-chats cheepin'
Or high in the hedge at dusk
A rogue of a blackbird wheepin'.
If I was in Castlewellan
There's be fiddlin' after the fair,
There's no dancin' on Slieve-na-man;
Och! it's lonely there.

Richard Rowley, in *Apollo in Mourne* (Belfast, 1978)

The Castle Castlewellan Co. Down

Ballynahinch - Spa

The Spa—Ballynahinch—Co Down

The prettiest little spot on earth, or mortal ever saw,
Is a mile or so from Ballynahinch and called by name—
  The Spa;
A health resort of diamond type, where Springs abound
  galore,
Once drink these crystal tonics, you'd ask for nothing
  more.

There you've got a hall divine in which to sing and pray,
Which gratifies the human eye to look at every day,
Right at its back there rears a manse where lives the holy
  Mac.
Whose father Adam owned us all—we can't deny this
  fact.

South of this hall of God-dom there stands a national
  school,
Where little folk are taught to write and read and feel
  the rule;
Beyond all winds a labyrinth so intricate and queer,
Within you must not enter if possessed of any fear.

As paths are strayed and crooked, they lead you here
  and there,
The more you try your exit, the deeper gets the lair;
For hours I've trodden on them, my mind a bower of
  dread
Lest I should get benighted and this labyrinth be my
  bed!

Once enter it your doom is cast unless a friend is nigh
To lead you in and out its crooks, and save you many
  a sigh.
Should you chance its centre to attain, a rustic house
  abides
Where the heart unfettered tells its joys, and all its
  sorrows hides.

'Twas there within this winding span of art, love came
  to me.
The day was fine and sunny for both butterfly and bee;
I'd lost my way, when forward came a gentleman
  from town,
Who proffered me assistance as he lead me round and
  round.

Its rustic heart arrived at, we sat down to chat and rest,
The moments crept to hours within this lovers' nest;
The clouds of heaven at last began to spread their
  greyish sails,
Above this bower of rural worth so many lovers hail.

We parted friends upon that day two links of love's
  bright chain,
Which afterwards were soldered into one, for now I reign
As Mrs. Maurice Mundy of fame and fortune fair
I'd stray within its nooks again to meet what I met there!

(cont'd)

Spa Church,
Ballynahinch

The Spa (cont'd)

The Spa is bounded on the north by an hotel of old,
But since its second baptism "Hydro" it's called I'm told,
Its east is pieballed here and there with trees and houses
  small,
Ending in a villa built which crowns the others all.

Its southern wing is bounded by this winding dream
  of old,
Whose zig-zag interior glad and sad tales oft has told;
Along its west stands nature, whose parasols so grand
Have often sheltered you and me from Sol's hot
  scorching hand.

Two springs of icy waters within its boundary lie,
One sulphur, and one iron to drink when you are dry;
There also is a ballroom, in which to dance and sing
And play a game of cards, or bridge, in fact play
  anything.

Refreshments too you'll find within this spacious room
  of note,
'Tis here your wants are all supplied from tea to table
  d'hôte;
For whisky, wine or brandy, to get these would you
  pinch,
You'd have to tramp to Walker's Hotel of Ballynahinch.

Take warning then my readers when sickness tries you
  sore,
Just pack your "alls" and off you go for health if
  nothing more
To the brightest little spot on earth, so don't have doubt
  or dread,
You'll ne'er regret a visit to this healthy northern bed.

You've got a decent lodging-house in old times called
  "Hotel",
But under perfumed management "Hydro" just does
  as well.
So any of my "patrons" who claim to be "select",
And seek a change this "Hydro" will your comfort well
  protect.

Your souls are soothed on Sundays by sermons choice and
  rare,
Your lungs are fed on week-days with rarest, purest air,
Your mind becomes a bower of ease and goodly thought,
Your strength will increase daily which to the Spa you
  brought.

Now "buck up" sickly sinners throughout this Isle of
  Saints,
Repair to where such bracing air will stay your grave
  complaints.
Think of the Spa—dream of it! the thought is not
  enough,
Ah! you must go—it fattens you—the Spa's the best of
  stuff.

Amanda McKittrick Ros, *Poems of puncture* (London, 1913)

Elmwood Spa, Ballynahinch.

The Spa

Archery Fête At Ballynahinch Spa

On Tuesday last, a rural *fête* was given by Mr. and Mrs. Ker, in the beautiful grounds at Ballynahinch Spa, the undulating effect of which added greatly to the scenery. About two o'clock, the company, which consisted of the *élite* of the surrounding neighbourhood, had arrived. The amusements were commenced by the Amateur Band of Killileagh playing the National Anthem, and many beautiful pieces of music, in a masterly style. Groups with happy countenances, promenaded through the improvements, which have been laid out with exquisite taste; and many old frequenters of the Spa, who have not been there since they were accustomed to see them long ago ''rude and rough'', could scarcely believe they were in the same region, or breathed the same atmosphere. Flags and many emblematical devices were tastefully displayed through the grounds, which, with two targets, placed at about thirty yards distant, indicated the additional attraction of the presence of the fair disciples of Cupid, who appeared in his armour, and the uniform generally adopted by Archery Societies, viz.— Polka jackets of green velvet, and silver buttons; book muslin dresses, with black boots; large leaved straw hats, looped on the right side with straw loop and button, and a bunch of roses, or other flowers, trimmed with a rosette of green and white ribbon, tied under the chin with same, together with a bow and quiver of arrows — of one of which societies this was intended to be the commencement. The fair competitors, twelve in number, took up their ground, and proceeded to discharge three arrows each round from their bows, under the kind instruction, guidance, and gallantry of Captain Philips, of the 44th Regiment, quartered in Downpatrick, who, with an affability and readiness to oblige, so happily blended with his military character, mainly developed the prowess of the the shortness of the notice, the little practice, and the inferior materials which some were only enabled to collect. The strings of many of the bows, having given way, could not be replaced, and occasioned a facetious remark, which we reiterate— 'that ladies should always have "two strings to their bow".' No accident occurred, except one of a very trifling nature. One of the ladies wounded a man who incautiously passed in the direction of the arrow; it perforated his hat, and merely scraped the skin. Several young gentlemen immediately exclaimed— 'Oh! how I envy that man!' There was a cow on the grounds, ornamented with garlands of flowers, for the purpose of affording milk for syllabub, and from the number who partook of that beverage, she was as able and willing to exercise the virtues of hospitality as her kind and generous owners. She was attended by a 'lady in waiting', dressed in a grotesque cap, petticoat, and skirt '*à la Suisse*'.

Belfast News-letter, 20 July 1847

It is interesting to note the date of this idyllic and gentlemanly feasting; for the rest of Ireland it is the time of the Great Famine.

Montalto, Ballynahinch

Newry

Men of Down!

They may tell you all too plainly
That they think your ways ungainly,
That your speeches seldom savour
Of a sycophantic flavour,
That you're all but blunt to rudeness
In your independent shrewdness,
   And to jibes they may subject you,
     Men of Down;
But I know your nature better,
Know you're truthful to the letter;
   Therefore I, for one, respect you,
     Men of Down!

They may point to other places,
Where the folk have smoother faces,
Where the women smile more coyly
And the tongues of men are oily,
Where they love to cringe and flatter
And with fulsome praise bespatter,
   And a rougher race may deem you,
     Men of Down;
But I know your silent action
Is worth all their loud attraction;
   Therefore I, for one, esteem you,
     Men of Down!

They may say you lack the graces
Of the poet in your phrases,
That a sentimental ranting
In your daily life is wanting,
And that Fancy's out of season
With your common-sense and reason,
   That no Delphic draughts inspire you,
     Men of Down;
But your earnest life's concealing
All the poet's deeper feeling;
   Therefore I, for one, admire you,
     Men of Down!

Yes, you don't go reeling blindly,
But you're true as steel, and kindly,
And your friendships ne'er grow colder;
And no soldiers' hearts are bolder,
And you scorn the braggart's tumour,
And you're rich in genial humour,
   And you're calm when sorrows strike you,
     Men of Down;
And you'll face the fiercest foeman,
And you'll bend your necks to no man;
   Therefore, high and low, I like you,
     Men of Down!

G.F. Savage-Armstrong, *Poems national and international* (Dublin, 1917)